Poetry for Kids

Emily Dickinson

POETRY FOR KIDS

Emily Dickinson

ILLUSTRATED BY
CHRISTINE DAVENIER

EDITED BY SUSAN SNIVELY, PhD

MoonDance

Quarto is the authority on a wide range of topics.
Quarto educates, entertains, and enriches the lives of our readers—
enthusiasts and lovers of hands-on living.
www.quartoknows.com

Publisher's Note

Many years ago, my grandmother read poetry to me at a very young age, even Shakespeare. She felt, as I now can appreciate, that the emotion and mood of poetry, even when it is almost too hard to understand, is so essential to understanding the world around us. I'm hoping that this series, with its selection of a very diverse group of poets, and with art by some of the world's best illustrators, will bring that all to life for a new generation. –Charles Nurnberg

MoonDance

6 Orchard Road, Suite 100
Lake Forest, CA 92630
quartoknows.com
Visit our blogs at quartoknows.com

Printed in China
1 3 5 7 9 10 8 6 4 2

MIX
Paper from
responsible sources
FSC® C101537

Contents

Introduction

EMILY DICKINSON WAS BORN ON DECEMBER 10, 1830, AND DIED ON MAY 15, 1886.

She lived in Amherst, Massachusetts, all her life, occupying a large brick house on Main Street near a huge meadow, the railroad station, and a hat factory. Two blocks away was Amherst College, which her grandfather Samuel Fowler Dickinson had helped to found in 1821. Emily's father, Edward, was a lawyer, treasurer of Amherst College, a member of the General Court of Massachusetts, and, briefly, a US congressman. He married Emily Norcross of Monson, Massachusetts, in May 1828. A quiet, sweet-natured woman, Emily Norcross was well educated and especially talented at gardening and baking. She and Edward had three children: Austin, born in 1829; Emily; and Lavinia, born in 1833. The smart, lively children shared a love of reading, music, nature, and each other's company.

Edward Dickinson helped to bring the railroad to the small town in 1853. Emily frequently heard the train's "horrid, hooting stanza," the whistles from the hat factory, and even the sounds of tumbling acrobats and caged animals moving along Main Street in the middle of the night when the circus came to town. The large windows of The Homestead showed Emily the dramas of the changing seasons and of life in "a country town."

The poet's life was both quiet and busy. She visited Washington, DC, and also journeyed to Philadelphia, Hartford, Worcester, Springfield, Boston, and Cambridge. Yet Emily Dickinson felt most comfortable at home. "Home is a holy thing," she remarked. She baked bread for the household, worked in the huge garden, wrote possibly ten thousand letters—think of what she might have done with e-mail!—and created poems that were unlike anybody else's poems: full of word-play, startling images, puzzles, and surprises.

In her mid-thirties, Emily developed a severe eye problem and was treated in Boston, where she stayed with her cousins Louisa and Frances Norcross. After "months of Siberia," she eventually improved. In 1874, her father, Edward, died unexpectedly of a stroke, and the following year, Emily's mother suffered a stroke that left her dependent on her daughters and their servant and friend Maggie Maher. Emily gradually withdrew from social activity, although she enjoyed visits from her good friends and baked gingerbread for the neighborhood children. The care of her mother, her devotion to writing poetry, and the pleasures of gardening took much of Emily's time.

Emily Dickinson's poems are populated by the birds, insects, frogs, snakes, and other creatures she observed on her property. Their activities, lives, and deaths seem like those of her relations. Her lifelong interest in science, especially botany and astronomy, enriched her language with beauty and wonder.

Emily died at age fifty-five in 1886, of hypertension, leaving behind a treasure trove of nearly 1,800 poems. In November 1890, her first volume, edited by Thomas Wentworth Higginson and Mabel Loomis Todd, was published, and went into eleven printings in one year. Now her readers can view her poems online (http://www.edickinson.org/), decipher her quirky handwriting, study the words she played with, and, as her sister, Lavinia, predicted, behold the poet's "genius."

Summer

It's all I have to bring today

It's all I have to bring today,
  This, and my heart beside,
This, and my heart, and all the fields,
  And all the meadows wide.
Be sure you count, should I forget,
  Some one the sum could tell,
This, and my heart, and all the bees
  Which in the clover dwell.

In the name of the Bee

In the name of the Bee —
And of the Butterfly —
And of the Breeze — Amen!

I'm nobody! Who are you?

I'm nobody! Who are you?
Are you nobody, too?
Then there's a pair of us — don't tell!
They'd banish us, you know.

How dreary to be somebody!
How public, like a frog
To tell your name the livelong day
To an admiring bog!

livelong — whole
bog — muddy swamp

A bird came down the walk

A bird came down the walk
He did not know I saw;
He bit an angleworm in halves
And ate the fellow, raw.

And then he drank a dew
From a convenient grass,
And then hopped sidewise to the wall
To let a beetle pass.

He glanced with rapid eyes
That hurried all abroad,
They looked like frightened beads, I thought;
He stirred his velvet head

Like one in danger; cautious,
I offered him a crumb,
And he unrolled his feathers
And rowed him softer home

Than oars divide the ocean,
Too silver for a seam,
Or butterflies, off banks of noon,
Leap, plashless, as they swim.

seam — ripple, furrow
plashless — smoothly, without splashing

They dropped like Flakes

They dropped like Flakes
They dropped like stars
Like Petals from a Rose
When suddenly across the June
A Wind with fingers goes

They perished in the seamless Grass
No eye could find the place
But God can summon every face
On his Repealless List.

flakes — snowflakes
stars — shooting stars, meteors
perished — died
seamless — without furrows
repealless — endless, from which
 nothing is erased

"Answer, July!"

"Answer, July! —
Where is the Bee —
Where is the Blush —
Where is the Hay?"

"Ah," said July,
"Where is the Seed —
Where is the Bud —
Where is the May? —
   Answer Thee me!"

"Nay," said the May,
"Show me the Snow —
Show me the Bells —
Show me the Jay!"

Quibbled the Jay,
"Where be the Maize —
Where be the Haze —
Where be the Burr?
   "Here!" — said the Year.

quibbled — answered
maize — corn
burr — seedpod

13

A narrow fellow in the grass

A narrow fellow in the grass
Occasionally rides;
You may have met him, — did you not?
His notice sudden is.

The grass divides as with a comb,
A spotted shaft is seen;
And then it closes at your feet
And opens further on.

He likes a boggy acre,
A floor too cool for corn.
Yet when a child, and barefoot,
I more than once, at morn,

Have passed, I thought, a whip-lash
Unbraiding in the sun, —
When, stooping to secure it,
It wrinkled, and was gone.

Several of nature's people
I know, and they know me;
I feel for them a transport
Of cordiality;

But never met this fellow,
Attended or alone,
Without a tighter breathing,
And zero at the bone.

shaft — dark, flash, snake
cordiality — friendly feeling
zero — freezing in the blood

15

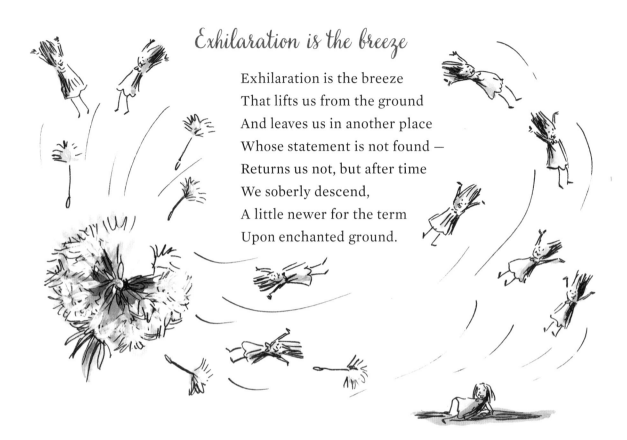

Exhilaration is the breeze

Exhilaration is the breeze
That lifts us from the ground
And leaves us in another place
Whose statement is not found —
Returns us not, but after time
We soberly descend,
A little newer for the term
Upon enchanted ground.

exhilaration — joy, imagination
statement — definite meaning

To make a prairie it takes a clover and one bee

To make a prairie it takes a clover and one bee,
One clover, and a bee,
And revery.
The revery alone will do
If bees are few.

prairie — meadow
revery — daydream

A soft sea washed around the house

A soft sea washed around the house,
A sea of summer air,
And rose and fell the magic planks
That sailed without a care.

For captain was the butterfly,
For helmsman was the bee,
And an entire universe
For the delighted crew.

helmsman — one who steers a ship

From all the jails the boys and girls

From all the jails the boys and girls
    Ecstatically leap, —
Beloved, only afternoon
    That prison doesn't keep.

They storm the earth and stun the air,
    A mob of solid bliss.
Alas! that frowns could lie in wait
    For such a foe as this!

ecstatically — with wild joy

Autumn

The gentian weaves her fringes

The gentian weaves her fringes,
The maple's loom is red.
My departing blossoms
    Obviate parade.

*gentian — purple wildflower
with white-fringed petals
obviate — prevent*

Faith is a fine invention

Faith is a fine invention
For gentlemen who see
But microscopes are prudent
In an emergency!

20

prudent — cautious and practical

Blazing in gold and quenching in purple

Blazing in gold and quenching in purple,
Leaping like leopards to the sky,
Then at the feet of the old horizon
Laying her spotted face, to die;

Stooping as low as the otter's window,
Touching the roof and tinting the barn,
Kissing her bonnet to the meadow, —
And the juggler of day is gone!

I never saw a moor

I never saw a moor.
I never saw the sea;
Yet know I how the heather looks,
And what a wave must be.

I never spoke with God,
Nor visited in heaven;
Yet certain am I of the spot
As if the chart were given.

moor — bog or marsh
heather — purplish plant that grows on moors
chart — map

He fumbles at your spirit

He fumbles at your spirit
  As players at the keys
Before they drop full music on
  He stuns you by degrees,

Prepares your brittle substance
  For the ethereal Blow
By fainter hammers, further heard,
  Then nearer, then so slow

Your breath has time to straighten
  Your brain to bubble cool, —
Deals one imperial thunderbolt
  That scalps your naked soul.

before they drop full music on — before they start playing
brittle — easily broken
ethereal — out of this world, mysterious
imperial — supreme, mighty

Because I could not stop for Death

Because I could not stop for Death,
He kindly stopped for me;
The carriage held but just ourselves
And Immortality.

We slowly drove, he knew no haste
And I had put away
My labor, and my leisure too,
For his civility.

We passed the school where children played,
Their lessons scarcely done;
We passed the fields of gazing grain,
We passed the setting sun.

We paused before a house that seemed
A swelling of the ground —
The roof was scarcely visible —
The cornice but a mound.

Since then 'tis centuries; but each
Feels shorter than the day
I first surmised the horses' heads
Were toward eternity.

leisure — play, relaxation
civility — courtesy, politeness
cornice — roof corner

The cricket sang

The cricket sang
And set the sun
And workmen finished one by one
Their seam the day upon.

The low grass loaded with the dew,
The twilight stood, as strangers do,
With hat in hand, polite and new
To stay as if, or go.

A vastness, as a neighbor, came,
A wisdom without face, or name,
A peace, as hemispheres at home,
And so the night became.

Winter

Safe in their alabaster chambers

Safe in their alabaster chambers,
Untouched by morning and untouched by noon,
Lie the meek members of the resurrection,
Rafter of satin and roof of stone.

Grand go the years in the crescent above them;
Worlds scoop their arcs, and firmaments row,
Diadems drop and Doges surrender,
Soundless as dots on a disc of snow.

alabaster — a pure white stone
resurrection — the revival of the dead
scoop — take out with a sweeping motion
firmaments — the sky or heavens
diadems — crowns
doges — rulers of Venice

It sifts from leaden sieves

It sifts from leaden sieves,
It powders all the wood,
It fills with alabaster wool
The wrinkles of the road.

It makes an even face
Of mountain and of plain, —
Unbroken forehead from the east
Unto the east again.

It reaches to the fence,
It wraps it, rail by rail,
Till it is lost in fleeces.
It flings a crystal veil

On stump and stack and stem, —
The summer's empty room,
Acres of seams where harvests were,
Recordless, but for them.

It ruffles wrists of posts,
As ankles of a queen, —
Then stills its artisans like ghosts,
Denying they have been.

leaden — gray and cold-looking
sieves — strainers

This is my letter to the world

This is my letter to the world,
    That never wrote to me, —
The simple news that Nature told,
    With tender majesty.

Her message is committed
    To hands I cannot see;
For love of her, sweet countrymen,
    Judge tenderly of me!

The spider holds a silver ball

The spider holds a silver ball
In unperceivèd hands
And dancing softly to himself
His yarn of pearl unwinds.

He plies from naught to naught
In unsubstantial trade,
Supplants our tapestries with his
In half the period —

An hour to rear supreme
His theories of light,
Then dangle from the housewife's broom,
His sophistries forgot.

unperceivèd — unseen
plies — works
naught — nothing
unsubstantial — unseen
tapestries — wall-hangings
sophistries — ideas

There's a certain slant of light

There's a certain slant of light,
On winter afternoons,
That oppresses, like the weight
Of cathedral tunes.

Heavenly hurt it gives us;
We can find no scar,
But internal difference
Where the meanings are.

None may teach it — Any —
'Tis the seal, despair, —
An imperial affliction
Sent us of the air.

When it comes, the landscape listens,
Shadows hold their breath;
When it goes 'tis like the distance
On the look of death.

oppresses — weighs down
imperial affliction — powerful pain or disturbance

The going from a world we know

The going from a world we know
To one a wonder still
Is like the child's adversity
Whose vista is a hill,
Behind the hill is sorcery
And everything unknown,
But will the secret compensate
For climbing it alone?

adversity — difficulty, struggle
vista — distant view
sorcery — witchcraft, magic
compensate — make up for

Like brooms of steel

Like brooms of steel
The Snow and Wind
Had swept the Winter Street,
The House was hooked,
The Sun sent out
Faint Deputies of heat–
Where rode the Bird
The Silence tied
His ample, plodding Steed,
The Apple in the cellar snug
Was all the one that played.

hooked — locked up
deputies — law-enforcers

I went to heaven

I went to heaven —
'Twas a small town —
Lit with a Ruby —
Lathed with down —
Stiller than the fields
At the full dew,
Beautiful as pictures
No man drew,
People like the moth
Of Mechlin frames —
Duties of gossamer
And eider names
Almost contented
I could be —
'Mong such unique
Society

lathed — covered
Mechlin frames — bodies made of fine lace
duties — clothing
eider — soft, like ducks' down
unique — one of a kind

Spring

New feet within my garden go

New feet within my garden go,
New fingers stir the sod;
A troubadour upon the elm
Betrays the solitude.

New children play upon the green,
New weary sleep below;
And still the pensive spring returns,
And still the punctual snow!

sod — earth
troubadour — old name given to a poet in France
betrays — upsets or reveals
pensive — thoughtful in a sad way
punctual — exact

Bee, I'm expecting you!

Bee, I'm expecting you!
Was saying yesterday
To somebody you know
That you were due.

The frogs got home last week,
Are settled and at work,
Birds mostly back,
The clover warm and thick.

You'll get my letter by
The seventeenth; reply,
Or better, be with me.
　　　Yours,
　　　　Fly.

Hope is the thing with feathers

Hope is the thing with feathers
That perches in the soul,
And sings the tune without the words,
And never stops at all,

And sweetest in the gale is heard;
And sore must be the storm
That could abash the little bird
That kept so many warm.

I've heard it in the chillest land,
And on the strangest sea;
Yet, never, in extremity,
It asked a crumb of me.

abash — cause to be silent, or frighten
sore — hard or fierce
extremity — severe hardship

Will there really be a morning?

Will there really be a morning?
Is there such a thing as day?
Could I see it from the mountains
If I were as tall as they?

Has it feet like water-lilies?
Has it feathers like a bird?
Is it brought from famous countries
Of which I have never heard?

Oh some scholar! Oh some sailor!
Oh some wise man from the skies!
Please to tell a little pilgrim
Where the place called "morning" lies!

pilgrim — a wanderer or traveler, especially to a holy place

39

A word is dead

A word is dead
When it is said
Some say.
I say it just
Begins to live
That day.

I send two Sunsets

I send two Sunsets —
Day and I in competition ran.
I finished two, and several stars,
While he was making one.

His own was ampler —
But, as I was saying to a friend,
Mine is the more convenient
To carry in the hand.

41

The wind begun to rock the grass

The wind begun to rock the grass
With threatening tunes and low, —
He flung a menace at the earth,
A menace at the sky.

The leaves unhooked themselves from trees
And started all abroad;
The dust did scoop itself like hands
And throw away the road.

The wagons quickened on the streets,
The thunder hurried slow;
The lightning showed a yellow beak,
And then a livid claw.

The birds put up the bars to nests,
The cattle fled to barns;
There came one drop of giant rain,
And then, as if the hands

That held the dams had parted hold,
The waters wrecked the sky,
But overlooked my father's house,
Just quartering a tree.

menace — threat or curse
livid — fiery
quartering — breaking into four pieces

A curious cloud surprised the sky

A curious cloud surprised the sky,
'Twas like a sheet with horns;
The sheet was blue, the antlers gray,
It almost touched the lawns

So low it leaned, then statelier drew,
And trailed like robes away —
A queen adown a satin aisle
Had not the majesty.

adown — moving down

There is no frigate like a book

There is no frigate like a book
    To take us lands away,
Nor any coursers like a page
    Of prancing poetry.
This traverse may the poorest take
    Without oppress of toll;
How frugal is the chariot
    That bears a human soul!

frigate — boat
coursers — powerful horses
traverse — travel
oppress — burden
frugal — careful with money

What Emily Was Thinking

Summer

It's all I have to bring today: Emily offers a gift that includes her heart, the fields and meadows, then "all the bees." She says "this, and my heart" three times, as if speaking a magic charm.

In the name of the Bee: Emily crafts a blessing from three happy words beginning with "B"—the Bee, the Butterfly, and the Breeze, who live in her garden.

I'm nobody! Who are you?: The poet, "nobody," makes friends with another nobody. Unlike the "dreary" somebodies who brag about themselves, Emily has sneaky fun with the rhymes of "frog" and "bog."

A bird came down the walk: Secretly watching a bird gobble his angleworm lunch, Emily captures his nervous movements. As he refuses her "crumb" and leaps into the air, the bird seems to swim in light.

They dropped like Flakes: During the Civil War (1861–1865), which happened in Emily's lifetime, young men were killed. The poet grieved for them. Many disappeared and were never buried. But God, she says, knows who they are.

"Answer, July!": The seasons go by quickly! When Emily asks July where spring has gone, May reminds July of winter and early spring blue jays. When the fussy blue jay mentions the fall harvests, mists, and seed-pods, the Year speaks up to claim them all.

A narrow fellow in the grass: The poet sees a snake creeping through the grass. She knows its home and habits, and makes her poem slither down the page. The last line shivers in its cold rhymes of "zero" and "bone."

Exhilaration is the breeze: Speaking the word "exhilaration" lets us walk on air, until we come back to earth, refreshed by a magical joy.

To make a prairie it takes a clover and one bee: The poet liked to bake sweet treats. Here is her recipe for a meadow. The secret ingredient is daydream.

A soft sea washed around the house: The poet imagines her house sailing on an ocean of summer air, guided by a butterfly and a bee. As part of the universe, she gets to ride along.

From all the jails the boys and girls: School's out! Children are free to run and make noise. It's too bad that grownups don't like the "mob."

Autumn

The gentian weaves her fringes: In fall, the poet sees her garden prepare for the cold by weaving bright cloth. When the flowers depart, their vivid parade ends.

Faith is a fine invention: In this sharp and sassy poem, Emily challenges "gentlemen" who see religion as superior to science. A microscope lets her examine hidden worlds.

Blazing in gold and quenching in purple: The active words in the poem—which end in "ing"—create a circus out of a sunset, commanded by the "juggler of day," the sun.

I never saw a moor: Although she doesn't know the world far from home, the poet has an imagination. She can shut her eyes and be wherever she wishes to go.

He fumbles at your spirit: The poet captures the noisy music of a thunderstorm, as if trapped inside a huge piano. The sounds heighten the drama, until the thunderbolt delivers its mighty blow.

Because I could not stop for Death: A kind carriage driver takes the poet from life to death, past childhood scenes. At sunset, she sees that her final "house" lies in the burying ground, and that the driver has taken her toward "eternity," where time disappears into the journey.

The cricket sang: A cricket's song helps the sun finish its daily work. When night descends, the day, like a life, has ended in peace. The poem's gentle rhymes—"name," "home,"—create a hymn of farewell.

Winter

Safe in their alabaster chambers: Emily sees both underground, where the dead sleep, and into space, where stars and planets move like ships rowing on a vast sea. Even powerful rulers disappear, like "dots" of snow on a white field.

It sifts from leaden sieves: The snow whirls through this poem like an acrobat, or a theatrical designer, transforming the landscape, then twirling into nothing.

This is my letter to the world: At her small writing table facing the large bright windows, Emily beholds the trees, grass, and sky, and then returns to her letter to the world. Her words carry her love of Nature in its simple majesty. We must read "tenderly."

The spider holds a silver ball: Like a poet, a spider works unseen, "dancing softly," as he constructs his whole world. But one sweep of a broom makes it vanish.

There's a certain slant of light: A beam of winter sunlight stabs the poet with "heavenly hurt." Then the "shadows" deepen the distance between herself and her memories of those she has lost.

The going from a world we know: When we wonder where we go when we die, we imagine climbing up a hill by ourselves. Mysteries await us, but will knowing their secrets be worth the lonely struggle?

Like brooms of steel: The winter wind and snow scrape the street like steel brooms. Silence stands tied to a tree, like a big farm-horse. But, safely stored for the winter, the apple plays in the cellar. Perhaps Emily wanted to be the apple.

I went to heaven: This heaven is so quiet and soft that its charms and moth-like people seem almost unreal. Having visited this heaven in a dream or poem, she might be "almost" contented there.

Spring

New feet within my garden go: In spring, Emily sees how new creatures—birds, animals, neighbors—arrive in town. She often thinks of opposites: the young and the "weary," the spring green and the same ground covered with snow.

Bee, I'm expecting you!: Here's a letter-poem from a fly to a bee, giving the neighborhood news. Like someone writing to an absent friend, the poet commands the friend to "be with me," making a pun on "be"!

Hope is the thing with feathers: The poet sees hope as a brave bird that sings through storm, cold, and loneliness, yet never asks to be fed "a crumb." The giving comes from hope, and the poet speaks in grateful awe.

Will there really be a morning?: Six questions in twelve lines! The poem is like a game of hide-and-go-seek, with sly Emily in her little-girl costume, teasing the "wise" grown-ups.

A word is dead: In twenty syllables, the poet lets her words hatch into life. The only two-syllable word, "begins," wakes up human speech and gives it a good "day."

I send two Sunsets: The poem offers a gift, perhaps of poems about sunsets and stars, written in a contest with "Day." The day's sunset is larger, but hers are easier to carry.

The wind begun to rock the grass: A thunderstorm upsets everything—grass, sky, wagons, birds, and cattle. Every line of the poem jumps with energy, until the house is spared and only a tree lies broken apart.

A curious cloud surprised the sky: Seeing a strange cloud with horns or antlers, the poet watches it descend, then arise and move off. When it changes shape, it looks like a queen walking on a satin carpet.

There is no frigate like a book: Reading a poem can take us anywhere in the world, and the journey is free. Emily's poems take us to China, Peru, Brazil—even past the earth into the stars.

Bibliography

Definitions of words and phrases in some of the poems are adapted from The Emily Dickinson Lexicon, Cynthia Hallen, ed. http://edl.byu.edu/index.php, 2007.

Hampson, Alfred Leete, ed. *Emily Dickinson: Poems for Youth.* Foreword by Mary Lamberton Becker. Boston: Little, Brown and Co., 1934.

Poems of Emily Dickinson. Selected by Helen Plotz. New York: Thomas Y. Crowell Co., 1965.

Todd, Mabel Loomis, and Millicent Todd Bingham, eds. *Bolts of Melody: New Poems of Emily Dickinson.* New York: Harper and Brothers Publishers, 1945.

Unpublished Poems of Emily Dickinson, edited by her niece Martha Dickinson Bianchi and Alfred Leete Hampson. Boston: Little, Brown and Co., 1936.

Index